CW00486012

RETIRED AT
25

THE LAW OF ATTRACTION

BEN COLE-EDWARDS

Text copyright © Ben Cole-Edwards 2021
Design copyright © Rebeckah Griffiths 2021
All rights reserved.

Ben Cole-Edwards has asserted his right under the Copyright, Designs
and Patents Act 1988 to be identified as the author of this work.

No part of this book may be reprinted or reproduced or utilised in any form
or by electronic, mechanical or any other means, now known or hereafter
invented, including photocopying or recording, or in any information
storage or retrieval system, without the permission in writing from the
Publisher and Author.

First published 2021
by Rowanvale Books Ltd
The Gate
Keppoch Street
Roath
Cardiff
CF24 3JW
www.rowanvalebooks.com

A CIP catalogue record for this book is available from the British Library.

Paperback ISBN: 978-1-913662-59-2
eBook ISBN: 978-1-913662-60-8

To Dad.

THE LAW OF ATTRACTION

Hi, my name is Ben Cole-Edwards, and I cannot believe that this book is in your hands. Firstly, I just want to say thank you for picking up a copy of this book; I'm truly honoured to know that my words have reached you. If this book is in your hands, that means everything you're about to digest and learn is one hundred percent true and that the Law of Attraction really does work. I have an infinite amount of faith and trust in the lessons that I am going to pass on to you. So much faith, in fact, that as I write this opening section on Wednesday the 22nd of July 2020, I have £4170 in the bank and £1500 in stocks. I am an online Personal Trainer, I work 20 hours a week in a supermarket and am a father-to-be. By the time I finish this book, I will have purchased my first property to rent out and have financial freedom for my family. Below, I will state the date on the day I finish this book and prove my teachings, and if this book is in your hands then all of my dreams have come true before publishing. *Bold move, Ben.*

Thursday, 22nd of April, 2021

Wow. Honestly, wow. It's absolutely crazy for me to read that opening statement. It honestly seems like I wrote it a lifetime ago. The proof is now in the pudding. It's true, it's all true. The Law of Attraction is THE way of life, and the Universe itself has become my best friend. The year I wrote that opening paragraph turned out to be the best and worst year of my life. I lost my grandfather just before starting this book, and shortly after I lost my father. Both of their deaths came as shocks to everyone in the family, but especially my father's at the age of 44, only 19 years older than myself. The biggest lesson that their passings taught me is that tomorrow is 100% not promised. People who die unexpectedly had plans for the next day and never knew their time was about to be up. I now understand that the key to a happy life is to appreciate each and every moment throughout each and every day, no exceptions. No doing things you don't want to, and no being anyone other than your true self. After their passings, I dove deep into the teachings that I am about to pass on to you in this book, and my life exploded in the best way possible. I cannot wait for you to read what I've put together for you.

I am now a father to a gorgeous little girl called Piper, and my life really is fantastic. There simply is nothing that I could possibly want to change. I left my supermarket job in February 2021 and stopped personal training as well, as it simply wasn't worth my time. The money I have made since November 2020, without even lifting a finger, makes my previous wages look like pennies. I'm now retired at 25—how bizarre is that?! I am well and truly blessed to live the life that I do, with pure financial freedom and the ability to spend every minute however I want, giving Piper, my family and myself the life we all deserve.

Please, take in every page of this book and use every single technique to your advantage until you find what works for YOU and allows you to immediately create the life of your dreams. I use the word 'immediately', because

I really did change my life so drastically in barely any time at all.

Within days, I began to see the effects of the teachings that I am passing on to you in this book. I manifested cars, health and even my daughter. I made a million pounds in 45 seconds and lost it even quicker. I have the freedom to do whatever I want, and the word 'stress' does not appear in my vocabulary. I cannot wait for you to implement the teachings of my book and to contact me to tell me how your life has changed overnight.

Just before we begin, I want to touch on the length of this book. I've read a lot of books since starting my journey, and although the wisdom I've received from them all has been extremely valuable and clearly worth more than its weight in gold, many were a lot longer than they needed to be. I've purposely kept this book short and sweet so you don't get bored with waffle. Each page contains valuable lessons. If I can teach you a lesson in one sentence, there's no point stretching it out over thirty pages.

Once again, thank you for taking the time to read my book, and I sincerely hope the life that you're currently living suddenly becomes the life you've been dreaming about.

***

I am dedicating this book to my late grandfather, Freddie (who I called Dad), who taught me an infinite amount of life lessons. He told me on a number of occasions that everything I've set my mind on, I've accomplished. I didn't know it at the time but that was the Law of Attraction, as clear as day.

I will continue to achieve what I set my mind on and teach others like you have taught me.

Thank you for sitting on my shoulder and guiding me through life.

I love you, Dad.

***

Retired at 25 is split into two parts. The first part is where you learn about lovely old me as I take you through my journey, my ups and downs, my wins and losses and how the Law of Attraction changed my life, almost quite literally overnight. The affirmations that I manifested will blow your mind and excite you to immediately create your own. Once we're best friends and you know all about me, you'll then move into the hands-on (more like brains-on!) second part of this book. This is where I've laid out all of the techniques that I used to get myself where I am today. You can pick any of the methods that you are going to read about to try for yourself. All you need is an open mind and a little faith.

To begin with, and with no beating around the bush, here's my story, of how I went from homeless at the age of nine to retired at 25.

I was born on the 10th of July, 1995, in a small town in South Wales called Maesteg. Nearly everyone in Maesteg worked a factory job, and 'aspirations' didn't seem to be in a lot of people's vocabulary. That's sadly still pretty much the case to this day. I've discovered over the last year that our sole purpose here on Earth is to seek joy, so if working in a factory keeps you happy and stress-free, that isn't an issue whatsoever. However, me being me, I craved more. I wanted to be different.

Growing up, I changed my mind a lot regarding what I wanted to do for the rest of my life. I wanted to work in a local toy shop, then I grew up a little. Then it was an astronaut, but I wasn't the best at science. Then at the age of 16, I wanted to be a Welsh teacher, but then I failed Welsh. For my A Levels, one of the subjects I studied was drama, which I thoroughly enjoyed throughout school, and I saw myself as the next Jim Carrey; I just loved making a fool out of myself on stage—or anywhere, for that matter—for others to laugh at. After achieving top marks, I went on to study acting at university, and although I made great friends and had a great time, the course just wasn't for me. I just wanted to get people laughing, but they had us doing ballet (which I was awesome at, actually), singing (which did make people laugh, to be honest) and theatre. After just over a year I decided to quit, and around a month later I got my first job: in a factory. My auntie got me the job in the television manufacturing factory she worked at, and my entire family was over-the-moon that I now had a 'job for life', even at £5.13 an hour! When I took my first self-employed position a few years later and earned £3000 in my first month, my family told me to 'get a stable job'. They obviously had my best interests at heart, but I desired more, constantly.

Anyway, I digress. *Good start, Ben.* My parents, Mark and Nicola—who met in a factory, actually—got married when I was two. They lived happily ever after for around six months before getting a divorce. Five years later, my mother met another man and had my sister, Tanisha. I can't remember how long he stayed around for, but it wasn't much longer than my own father.

My mother hasn't had good relationships with men and has had an even worse relationship with money. I started off exactly like her when it came to money. I was nine years old when we lost our home due to my mother being unable to pay the mortgage. To be completely honest with you, I didn't know what we were then living in was a hostel until a good number of years later. I just thought it was a hotel, with one room. When I was ten, we moved into a council house, around two miles away from our last house. From that point—and even in our old house, actually—my mother was barely at home. Being a single mother-of-two working in a factory on an awful wage meant she was at work for most of the day just to provide a roof over our heads. Money was so tight that when it wasn't raining, she'd walk ten miles to and from work just to save money on fuel. I can see now why she wasn't at home, but growing up I'd have to stay at home throughout the holidays to look after my sister until my mother got back in the afternoon. During snowy days, I could hear my mates outside in the fields having fun and I'd be stuck in. That was shit.

We have a weird relationship, my mother and I. When we lived in our first home, she would go to work early and my grandmother would come to the house to get us ready for school. My grandmother would take us to school, pick us up from school, and then we'd stay at her house until my mother came home from work. On Wednesdays and over the weekend, I'd be over my other grandparents' house, so to be honest, I didn't spend much time with my mother. I'm not doubting her parenting abilities in the slightest, as she was only working for her children, but we had more of a brother-and-sister type of relationship—I'd tell her off just as much as she'd tell me off. Part of me still thinks that we didn't have the typical mother-and-son relationship because I looked so much like my father, and she hated him!

So, Ben, why are you telling us about your mother? I want to know how you made your fortune!

My mother was awful with money for as long as I can remember, partly because she wasn't earning much but also because she didn't know how money really works. Neither did I, until this year. My mother would go to work in the morning and say, 'If anyone knocks, don't answer it'—meaning there'd be companies knocking about money being owed. I remember opening the door one day to a man explaining that our washing machine was rented and my mother owed him £20!

You'll be happy to know that my mother is now a massive fan of the Law of Attraction (which was already working for her) and is also an investor in the stock market! Let's hear a congratulations!

I started an internal process in the television factory that I'd end up repeating at every job I would go on to work at. I'd get the job, nail my probation period, and then get hungry for more. I'd always see each job as easy, boring and repetitive and I'd then approach my boss and say, 'Look, I can do a lot more than this.' This would plant a seed in their heads that would make them think of me when a promotion opportunity arose. After my boss understood my potential—and in some cases, actually promoted me—I'd get bored and look for my next job! I think I've done this in literally every job I've had. In the end, I realised that I actually wanted less responsibility but more money, so that's what I eventually set out to achieve.

After being promoted, I went from my first factory job to my next, which was nearly double the pay but only a temporary position. My first boss pulled me to the side once I'd put my notice in and said, 'Do you really want to leave a permanent job for a temporary one? I know you don't like being on £5.13 an hour, but in two years when you're 21, you'll be on £6.21!' They've since shut down.

At that point in my life, every single penny I earned was blown on cars. I've had 26 cars at the time of writing this sentence, but it'll be 28 by the time I finish the book! If I earned £800 a month in my first job, I'd be looking for a £600 car on payday, putting new wheels on it, spraying the bumpers, and then not having enough money to put fuel into it… literally. At that time too I'd be posting the cars on social media, acting like I was rich!

Fast forward to my third factory job, and I still had no idea how money worked, tried steroids and ended up getting promoted after publishing my first crime/thriller novel. What a year… Taking steroids wasn't good for my mental health, let alone physical, my book barely made any money, and I got bullied in work most days! This whole 'phase' is still a blur, to be completely honest. I think it was midway through this job when I competed in my first fitness modelling show. I remember putting a video up online of my posing routine. I panicked as I posted it, scared to show people what I was doing. The same week, a group of people in work posted their own video mocking me. However, I am now literally financially free and they still work there. I'm not one to hold a grudge, but I'll admit, it is nice watching them drive past me on their way to work whilst I'm heading to the beach in my Range Rover Sport. Some of them even became personal training clients of mine. Imagine being bullied by someone who later goes on to pay you to help them! Karma is lovely.

At this point in my life, my roughly fifteenth car, which I think was my fourth VW Golf, was falling apart and leaking water. My mother said, and I quote, 'Instead of buying cheap cars all the time, why don't you take out a loan and buy a decent one?' My eyes lit up at this point. A loan? Money? *I* could get a loan? The thought of getting one would've never crossed my mind, but then I was hooked—it sounded like free money to me. Later that evening, my mother suggested taking out a £2000 loan, but at that point I was cash hungry. As the bank still classed me as a student since quitting uni, it was surprisingly easy to get accepted for a loan, so I applied for one and it hit my account two days later: £10,000. Believe me when I say I thought I was rich. I bought a £5000 car (worth £3000 max.), spent £1500 on it, sold it 6 months later for £2500, had tattoos done, booked a holiday and spent £1500 on vets bills for my dog who was ill at the time. And just like that, the loan was gone. I'd have to pay £269 a month for five years, and I'd spent it straight away. I can even recall posting a photo on social media of Leonardo DiCaprio in the scene from *The Wolf of Wall Street* where he's throwing money off his yacht. I captioned the photo with 'If you think you're bad with money, I just blew £10,000 in three weeks!' What the fuck?! Why did I do that? Actually, I did it to impress people. I had left university and wanted my friends there, along with everyone else I knew, to think that I was doing good. Well, I wasn't. #socialmedia

Here's where things get a little better. So, around 2016, I had left a bad relationship, got kicked out of my mother's house, moved into my father's house, got kicked out of my father's house, moved back into my mother's house and was still on steroids. No, seriously, it does get better. I was in a really, really bad place mentally at this time of my life, and remember meeting up with two mates. We sat down in McDonald's to have a chat, and they told me that I needed help, but I didn't think I did. I told them that I had two options: I was either going to get a one-way ticket to Thailand and live homeless on a beach, or kill myself and start over again. I genuinely thought they were good choices too. I think the only reason I didn't do anything stupid was because of my sister.

The steroids didn't help at all, either. I found that they really heightened my emotions. If I was happy, I was ecstatic, but if I was sad, I was depressed.

Okay, *so now* it gets better—I was lying when I said that before. I also lied when I said there would be a 'little' background info on my life at the start of the book. At the end of 2016, I met Jessica, my now fiancée—and potentially by the time you read this, my wife. We have the same birthday, so to me, it was fate. A lot of people call their significant others 'Angel', but Jess truly is one and I believe she saved my life.

2017 was the year that I quit my job. I had been promoted into the offices of the warehouse I worked in and had a LOT of responsibilities. However, I was never taken seriously. The office was full of experienced, mainly middle-aged people in shirts and trousers, and then I rocked up in a tracksuit, covered in tattoos and half their age. The thing was, I was brilliant at that job. There were only two of us in the whole place who could do my job, and we shared it. There were two or three people I got on with, but the rest; we just didn't click. I was in charge of a lot of things, and if the other person on the job wasn't in work and I'd decided not to work (even though I never did) then the whole place couldn't work. They didn't quite see that, though! They promised me a pay rise to the standard wage to go with the job, but they kept coming up with excuses not to for over a year. If someone came in on a night shift and it was their first ever day on the lowest paying job in the entire warehouse, they'd be on one pound more an hour than me!

My boss finally decided to put me on a salary instead of being hourly paid, but it actually worked out as less money because of all the overtime I was doing! That was when I'd had enough.

After competing in a fitness modelling show and not even placing (after telling everyone I was going to win), I received my stage photos. I had been training since I was 17 years old and was now 21. At that point, I'd learned how to gain muscle, lose weight, gain weight, get stronger and knew exactly what to eat to achieve certain goals. I had also helped a few friends get into shape too and started learning how other people's bodies worked and responded to certain training and nutrition. This was when I started down a new route as a Personal Trainer. I'd picked up my first dumbbells at around the age of 16 and had a gut feeling then that I wanted to be a Personal Trainer—one of my many goals, anyway.

I posted a few stage photos on my social media platforms and stated that I was 'now taking on *more* clients', even though I didn't have any, or any qualifications, in fact! I also posted a progress photo of one of my mates to show that I already had 'clients'. This took off for me like I never thought it would. Everyone still made fun of me at work, even more so now. One guy came up to me laughing and saying that I had no qualifications and wouldn't be able to do it. Just to note—between then and the time of writing this sentence, I've taken on 550 online clients, and that guy still hates his same job in the same factory. I took on one one-to-one client and one online client within the first day or two. The office job was giving me around £1200 a month, the one-to-one client was £200 a month, and I was charging £30 for an online plan. I'd be up at 6 a.m., work from seven to three, train my client, then myself, and then by the time I'd get home I was ready for bed! Sure, I was making more money, but I definitely wouldn't call it 'living'.

So here's when I took the leap of faith! I took on another one-to-one client and decided that I no longer needed or wanted to work in the office. I took a demotion, back to stacking orders for fifteen hours a week. I then got busier and busier and ended up quitting my job! I was making around £1200 a month on a good month just doing one-to-ones, and I worked the hours that I wanted and also chose who I wanted to work with! Being a one-to-one trainer with the occasional online client was great, while it lasted. I had also recently launched a clothing brand and put all my money into it, so I had zero spare funds and didn't prepare for what was to come! Also, I found myself in a predicament. I was charging £10 for an hour session, which meant that I was limited with my earning potential. Even if I worked 12 hours a day, seven days a week; I still wouldn't be able to scale the business. Always wanting more…

Christmas was around the corner, and out of nowhere, clients just started dropping out. Each client had a perfectly good explanation as to why they no longer wanted to train, but I just hadn't factored that into my income as I shovelled it all into the clothing brand. For me, however, that was it, I was done for! I had no money and not enough clients to cover bills, and long story short, I ended up in a call centre. Not a factory job, I hear you say? I'm a big people-person so I loved talking to customers, but ringing people up at 9 a.m. asking them if they'd like internet security for £2 a month just didn't vibrate on the same frequency as me. I spent three months there before finding a job delivering parcels for nearly double the money I was on!

Okay, so this is it! I thought. A self-employed position, company van and earning anywhere between £2000-£3000 per month—fantastic! I rolled up to my interview, which turned out to just be an 'induction day'—anyone could get the job. This was a great-paying job with a big firm, so I arrived in a suit. The five other boys were in tracksuits. They took us all on (besides one who failed the drug test) and handed us keys to our own vans, just like that! I started this job in the summer, so I was driving out in the sun in gorgeous areas, wearing shorts and a vest, listening to tunes and catching half a tan; I loved it! The boss took a liking to me and gave me his own company van. I remember him telling me how nice it was to drive and not like the others. Honestly, you should've seen his face when I totalled it three weeks later...

'Hi, mate. It's Ben.'

'What's up?'

'Well, I've had a little bump in the van.'

'How little?'

'Well, the van is in the middle of the road blocking both ways, and won't move as the front right arm has completely snapped off.'

I'm great with cars, but the other car was so badly damaged that even I couldn't tell what model it was. I'd had no seatbelt on and came out of the side window, and if there's ever been a time in my life where I've had to question how the fuck I'm still alive, that was it. All my fault, too.

After a week or so, they decided that they could only keep me on the team if I had my own van. I borrowed money from my fiancée to buy a £1500 Transit, and over the next month it broke down five times, resulting in me having to quit.

This was in 2018, and it wasn't long after that Jess and I moved out. We were quite lucky actually, in the sense that we rented off her mother in Jess's grandparents' old home. I managed to get another delivery job straight away. A mate of mine from the first job recommended me, and he left out the bit about the crash. This job wasn't too bad actually, once I got into it, but less money and I wouldn't know if I was working on any given day until the day before. So, as you guessed it, I didn't last long.

AND FINALLY, MY LAST ACTUAL JOB!

I saw an advert for a job in a small supermarket that was a three minute drive from our home, and I even sold my car shortly after getting the job because I wanted to save money on fuel. I arrived at the interview after applying for a 30 hours per week position, and the boss said, 'No one thinks this is a full-time job, do they?' I was the only one to say yes. He then went on to explain that they'd made a mistake when advertising the vacancy and that it was only actually 16 hours a week. Nevertheless, I got the job (and begged each week for overtime). At this exact time of writing, I have handed my notice in, all thanks to the Law of Attraction.

So here I am, a father who no longer works or takes on any clients because I'm financially free. What the fuck. In January 2020, I had £200 in the bank and by December I had £200,000. This wasn't luck, this wasn't hard work, this was me, creating my life from within myself.

I have written the opening to this book to show you that I was your average person, living an average life, doing average things. Throughout the rest of this book, I will tell you exactly how I manifested my own life, including my financial freedom, my happiness, my business growth—and even my own daughter. Honestly, I know you've probably purchased this book because you saw it online and thought, 'Hmm, I want to retire young', but if you really take in every single thing I'm about to tell you, your life will emotionally explode and you'll 'wake up' and understand that everything you see and experience in your life is created within your own mind. Most days, I catch a glimpse of myself in the mirror and I stop and stare into my own eyes and just think, 'Who the fuck are you? What the fuck are you?' By the end of this book, after implementing all the techniques, you'll want to do the same, and you'll come to realise that we aren't human beings that occasionally have spiritual experiences; we are spiritual beings that are temporarily living through a human experience. That went rather deep, rather fast, didn't it?

***

So there I was, welcoming in the year 2020. I had ZERO idea that this year was going to be the best and worst year of my life. At the start of the year I was doing around 25 hours at work and I was no longer training clients one-to-one. I was fully online, taking on around one or two clients per week, on a good week. This went well for a while, and I must've been earning around £1500 a month but working less in the supermarket, which was the goal. Then, at the end of February, I became a qualified Massage Therapist. I spent my last £200 buying furniture and decorations to renovate our spare room and turn it into my massage studio; this was on Friday the 13th of March. All was well, and I was so excited to lower my hours in work to do more massages and in effect make more money by working fewer hours.

That night, I had a phone call saying that my grandfather Freddie had collapsed in the bathroom against the door. My grandmother couldn't get in, so I headed there as quick as I could (luckily, we lived really close) and jumped through the bathroom window. My grandfather was more of a father to me growing up and taught me so much about everything. It was ME who had to come to the realisation that my grandfather was no longer in the body in front of me; it was the first time in my life I'd had to go through something like that. I performed CPR until the paramedics came, and after an hour they managed to get his heart started again, but he couldn't breathe on his own and wasn't responsive. We got to the hospital, and the doctor told us that there was an extremely low chance of him coming back and even if he did, he wouldn't be the same and would have zero quality of life. She explained that the best thing to do was to wait for his heart to start stopping again and let him go. My mother and I sat there beside him as we waited for the rest of the family to arrive, and once the machine started beeping, a nurse came over and informed us that that was it, he was going. Within seconds, he was gone.

Freddie had been the head of the family. Around two years earlier he'd been in hospital, and we'd thought it was his time then. He'd said to me, 'Remember, Ben, when I'm no longer the man, you're the man.'

I had around five weeks off work, and the flashbacks lasted a lot longer. I think it was around two weeks after my grandfather passed that the UK went into lockdown. What a strange time in my life. Freddie was loved by so many, but we could only have ten people at the funeral.

It was at this time that I started to read every day. I knew *why* I wanted to read, but not *what* to read, if that makes sense. I started by purchasing three books, and at this point each book was a lot of money for me. I purchased the following:

Just F*cking Do It - Noor Hibbert
Think and Grow Rich - Napoleon Hill

The Law of Attraction, The Teachings of Abraham -
Esther and Jerry Hicks

I bought the first book to improve my mindset, the second book to improve my financial situation, and the third to learn about the Law of Attraction. One of the first moments in my life when I 'clicked' was once I got halfway through the last book and realised they were all about the Law of Attraction. Three books that I'd bought for three different reasons were all about the same thing.

The main thing that stuck was the title of Napoleon Hill's book: *Think and Grow Rich*. I'd been reading the title wrong the whole time whenever I'd seen the book recommended online. In my opinion, it shouldn't be read as 'Think and Grow Rich' but more as 'Think. And Grow Rich'. The author talks about some sort of secret throughout the book that each successful person he interviews understands: You must first 'think'—which, in this sense, means to believe it to be true in your head first for it to then happen in reality. You must think (and know it to be true) about you growing rich, and then you *will* grow rich. Believe it within and it will all unravel for you in your physical life. I really hope that gives you a different understanding of the title, too.

If you think this is all mumbo-jumbo, and you're thinking, 'Okay, Ben, cool, you're basically Buddha, but I want to become rich.'—this mindset, if you will, that I've just explained is what let me turn £6700 into £200,000 in the last five weeks of the year, eight months after reading those three books. Honestly, that took zero hard work to do, too.

Okay, so it's summer and you're almost caught up—congrats on making it this far. So we're in lockdown and we're not allowed to leave the house unless it is absolutely essential. This was when I really got into my stride with reading and was nailing a book every week. We had a great few weeks of weather, and I made the most of it by getting up early, grabbing a book and heading out the back garden with the dogs. Have I mentioned the dogs yet? The day we moved in was the day we picked up our first French Bulldog, Romeo. Around seven months later we picked up another and called him Cooper. No idea why I told you that, but since you now know me…

So yeah, nailing books, loving the sun and trying my best to come to terms with my grandfather passing. This is when I started reading more and more about the term 'manifesting'. Like, so, you want me to write down what I want on a piece of paper and it'll just come true? Really? I'm super open-minded, but come on—it can't be that easy. I gave it a go, however, and here I am, writing what I've learnt in a book so you can learn too and immediately take control of your life.

This book is going to go really deep, really quick again here, but listen up! The Universe is working with you like a literal spiritual best friend, and all it wants is for you to get what you want. Please read that again. If you're thinking, 'Ah, here's another guy with a screw loose,' you're probably right actually, but remember that up until 2020 I was living every day skint, going from job to job with no idea how money worked and, to put it plainly, not having a good time, dude. Now, I can literally buy whatever I want, and I spend every single day happy, doing whatever I want. And the reason I'm currently sitting at my dining table, listening to Rocketman and tapping away on my keyboard is so that YOU—yes YOU—can do it all too! Even if Elton John isn't your thing.

So, what did I manifest first? I really wanted an Audi R8 but I had like zero money, so there was no point trying to manifest that, was there? Okay, so money. Let's start with money! All the books I was reading stated that you didn't need to wait and that everything can happen straight away. This sounded really farfetched to me, to be completely honest, but once again, I gave it go. I did exactly what the books taught me and started by creating the feeling in my head that money was coming my way, and had the figure of around £1000. When manifesting, being specific is key, and I was far from it. I didn't write anything down, I didn't have a specific figure nor a specific date I wanted to achieve this by, but I firmly believed it. Was I going to take on loads of clients in one go? That was all I could think of, unless I did a ton of overtime in work, but that wouldn't really add up. Over the next few days when reading, I kept the thought in my mind that the money was coming. One morning, not long after, I received an email from the government. My initial thought was, 'Great, how much money do I owe?' The email stated that as I was self-employed (as well as employed), I'd be entitled to a grant due to being unable to work because of the virus. I received £1046.

Right. Ben. Did that just happen? Did you just manifest £1046? Was it a coincidence? But all the books teach that there are no coincidences.

Okay, back to the books! How did I manifest the money without actually writing anything down? Is it just stronger when writing it down? Around this time I believe I was reading a book by Vex King, called *Good Vibes, Good Life*. This was yet another book that I'd had no idea was about the Law of Attraction and manifesting. I read about how Vex tried manifesting £500 (I believe) to be able to afford to go on a holiday with his mates. A few days before the cut-off date for him to add himself onto the holiday, he received a tax rebate through the door, to the sum of £500.

Okay, Ben, let's try again. I had around £1500 here, and there was this Audi A4 that I wanted, and every time I saw it advertised, the price kept coming down. The last time I read, the price was around £2500 so I tried to manifest it. I also tried to be more specific this time around. I still didn't give myself a date to achieve the goal by, nor did I write it down. I closed my eyes and imagined a silver Audi A4 outside my house. I did this for two or three minutes a day for a handful of days, and then one day I looked out the window and parked right outside my house was a silver Audi A4. Crazy. I was gobsmacked but also laughed, partly because of how it had actually worked and partly because it wasn't actually mine. The car stayed outside my house for three or four days before disappearing. One day I was leaving the house the same time as my next-door neighbour, and she pointed at the Audi and said, 'Do you know whose car that is?' I laughed and said no and that I was wondering the same thing!

I could see that the manifestation had worked, but not exactly how I'd planned it. The next page I read, maybe that same day or the morning after, stated that you need to be *really* specific when manifesting, and the author described that if you want a new car, you can't just imagine the car itself. You need to see yourself *inside* the car, holding the keys, starting the car, the smell of the interior, the feel of the seats! I wasn't manifesting myself in the car, or even the car being in my possession. I was simply imagining the car being in my street, and it was, bizarrely. I also found it crazy that whenever I'd have a question regarding the Universe or found myself in a particular situation, I could pick up a book and find the answer in the next page or two, every time!

I started thinking about the Universe itself and who I was actually manifesting to. Was I even doing it *to* someone? With someone? Someone or something? At this point, I can confirm that the Universe has *always* been working with you, you've just never put a name to it. The Universe, God, the Higher Being, whatever you want to call it, is part of you and you are a part of it, whether you like it or not. We are all one—you, I and the Universe itself. Told you it'd get deep.

Now it was time to take it up a notch and see how much difference it would make to my manifestations if I actually started writing them down instead of just thinking of them. A key point that I learned was to write them down in present tense and to write them amongst things that *are* already true. For example, 'I have an Audi R8' instead of, 'I *want* an Audi R8'. This has a ton of benefits. The main one is that your brain doesn't know the difference between what's real and what's not, so writing things down like this and reading them out tricks your brain into thinking you've already achieved something when you haven't. I know that sounds strange, but trust me. The second reason you want to write them down in this way is because the Universe only knows what you desire from what you tell it and how you feel it within. If you write down and manifest to the tune of 'I want more money', you're only telling the Universe that you have a lack of something, and therefore the Universe will just bring you more 'lack of', because that's what you're explaining. It goes something like this:

You: I have a big house with a sea view.

Universe: Okay, great, that's a normal statement, I love sea views too. I'll try my best to continue making that your reality.

OR

You: I want a bigger house.

Universe: Okay, so the vibe I'm getting here is that you're unhappy with your current situation, so I'll continue to make that your reality.

Like attracts like.

The best way to put it is that it's like how if you wake up in a bad mood, you have a bad day. You might wake up with a headache. You might check your phone and see an unexpected bill has taken you into your overdraft. You might stub your toe. You might have slept late and missed your alarm. Whatever the reason, due to a minor inconvenience in the morning, the rest of your day is always pretty shit, isn't it? On the other hand, have you ever woken up to great news? That refund you were expecting has gone in? Your new outfit for tonight's party has arrived, and it fits great? You've just started a business and you've woken up to a few orders? Great! You know where this is going, but the rest of your day goes absolutely swimmingly, doesn't it? Payday? On a high all day! Monday morning and you hate your job? Dreadful day.

Why are you telling me this, oh Mighty Ben? I'm telling you this to show you that the Law of Attraction has already been working for you. You woke up in a bad mood and subconsciously told the Universe that you hate today and everything is out to get you. What did the Universe do? It delivered! You woke up in a fantastic mood and looked forward to the day? The Universe then thought, 'Wow, this dude loooves his life, let's give him more of that!'

Once you truly feel the Universe as it unravels your desires in front of you, you'll have the power to stop the sad train. After really immersing myself into all of this and really connecting to the Universe, I can now jump out of a bad mood and straight into a good one, despite the circumstance. Maybe I've been in work and something has happened that has really affected me mentally. Perhaps I've had a text that has really got to me, or a customer has said something personal like, 'Why are you working here? I thought you were doing really well?' That one hurt my ego. However, regardless of what has happened to put me in a bad mood, I stop what I'm doing and ask myself: What emotion *are* you feeling right now? *Why* are you feeling this? What *could* you be happy about right now if you wanted to? And if none of that works, I listen to music and dance; you literally can't be unhappy whilst busting a move.

So, writing down my manifestations. I started with the only place I knew that I could potentially make more money, online personal training. At this point in time, taking on one or two online clients a week was amazing for me, but as always, I wanted more.

My first list of manifestations went something like this:

- I am Ben Cole-Edwards
- I am successful
- I am wealthy
- I have two healthy dogs, Romeo & Cooper
- I have an Audi R8
- I have the perfect relationship with Jess
- I take on one client every day
- I am happy
- I have made it

I would read this over every morning and repeat it in my head in the shower when getting ready for work. When in the shower, I would hold my arms out in front of me and physically pretend to pull these things into myself and really start to feel my own words. I'll explain that later.

Within a week, I was consistently taking on one client a day, no questions asked, not a day missed. This was when I really got into the flow of things. After a while, I was in the shower manifesting and went over my, 'I take on one client every day'. I then paused and thought, 'Actually, this *is* really true. I'm not pretending I've got something. I'm not trying to trick my brain into thinking that I take on one client a day, I *do* take on one client every day. What the fuck?!' I could really feel my inner frequency begin to vibrate even higher (we'll go over that later, too). So I upped it. 'I take on TWO clients every day.' It happened. Then, 'I take on THREE clients a day', and lo and behold! Throughout June and July I was taking on 10-12 clients every single day, and I got so caught up I'm sure I even stopped manifesting. I was only charging £45-£65 per diet plan, so I went from making £90-£120 a week to roughly £500 a day, on top of working in the supermarket and doing a few massages each week!

Jess and I had been trying for a baby for a few months by then, and we were trying everything we could. She was taking tablets that she'd bought online, we were both dieting, I'd stopped drinking energy drinks. I started to think it may have been the steroids, and she was beginning to blame it on her old birth control. I remembered taking steroids for longer than I should have at one point—had that ruined my chance of being a father? You won't (though you probably will, at this point) believe what I'm about to say. I wrote a new list of manifestations. I'm Ben, blah blah, I own an Audi R8, blah blah, Jess is pregnant. We caught that week, and as I finish this paragraph, our daughter, Piper, is due in four weeks and five days.

I was over the moon that Jess was finally pregnant, because all I'd ever wanted was my own family. The day we had the positive result I told everyone, despite Jess telling me to keep it a secret until week twelve. I just couldn't contain my excitement. From the moment we'd started trying, I'd spend hours watching pregnancy reveal videos and cry my eyes out, thinking of ways I could reveal it to my family. There was no cute reveal, however—I literally told them all within five minutes of doing the test. I phoned my mother and said, 'Hi Nanna.' Great surprise, Ben.

I was devastated that my grandfather wouldn't be here to meet my daughter, but I felt very connected to him spiritually by then and knew he was with me.

Through July and August, I started to get flashbacks to the night I had climbed through the bathroom window and saw my grandfather. I couldn't get it out of my head. I had never experienced a death in the family before, and so I phoned the doctor to see if it was normal or if I needed help. I started getting better though, for a while. Not long after, I had a phone call from my mother saying that she was suicidal and was 'thinking of ways not to be here'. I took a few days off work again due to stress, and my mother was a lot better not long after. This was probably the most stressful time of my life... so far.

For reasons that aren't really relevant, I wasn't speaking to my father for most of 2020 (we were like that—best friends one month, arguing the next). Then one day, at the end of August, Jess and I were sitting at the dining table and I had a phone call. The caller ID said it was my father and I let it ring. I looked at Jess and said he's probably calling to apologise now that my grandparents have told him that we're having a baby. I then had a voicemail. I told Jess, 'Watch this—it's going to be him saying, "It's me, call me."' Just as he'd usually do before we'd make up. I pressed play on the voicemail and put it on speaker. A woman's voice screamed, 'Ben, it's Stephanie next door, come down quick, Dad's dead.'

44 years old with no cause of death. He just died. My stepmother found him in the morning and he'd been dead for hours. I got there as quick as I could, and by the time I did, the paramedics had stopped attempting to revive him. I went to see him in the Chapel of Rest, just like I did with my grandfather, and it was no easier. I told him what I'd told him on the day he died when I saw him then. I apologised for some reason, I told him I loved him, I thanked him and then said that I wouldn't be able to see him for about 60 years until we were to meet again.

How crazy, and what a year. 25 years old and I had lowered my grandfather into the ground and cremated my father, within five months of each other. The two people who'd told me all the time how proud they were of me, gone, and not going to meet my daughter. Hardest year of my life.

Like I've said, I'm great at switching up my mood completely, but fuck me it suddenly got a lot harder.

Around October time I was really busy with massages, slightly quieter with online clients and working around 11 hours a week in the supermarket. Even though I had (and still have) my moments, which is completely healthy, I had come to terms with the deaths of my father and grandfather and truly began to feel them both with me every single day. I had around £6000 and was proudly updating my family of my savings at each £1000. In an ideal (but seemingly unrealistic) situation, I wanted

£10,000 behind me before the baby arrived. I ended up reaching around £8000 saved but was working quite a lot, and then took Jess to Cyprus when it was legal to travel to certain places—never thought I'd have to say that! We ever so slightly redecorated the house and bought Piper more clothes than she would ever need, and that brought my savings down to around £6000.

My manifestations were still there at this point but not as strong and not as often practised as before, because I was content. Towards the middle of November, I had £6700 in the stock market and maybe £500-£1000 in cash. I felt rich here, too. It actually sounds rather risky, looking back, because I could very well have lost my proudly saved money within an instant. However, if it hadn't worked, I wouldn't be typing these words and you wouldn't be reading them.

I started buying stocks with companies that we all know, to play it safe, but I have zero patience and barely broke even and ended up putting it all into one company, which was even riskier. I had zero knowledge of the stock market, couldn't (and still can't) read a chart and had just thrown my savings into a Chinese company that made electric cars, at $27 per share. I literally searched the name of the company on social media and thought, 'Hmm, this looks promising,' without even knowing what 'promising' meant in relation to stocks. Two weeks later and I had made £2000 profit and was over the moon! I was telling people at work how great this stock was and that they should get in as 'This is valued at $300!', which came from one person's post that I'd seen online! I genuinely thought I'd be set with this one stock. In my head, I was thinking that if this goes from $27 to $300 then I'd have like £74,000 which would feel like millions!

On the 27th of November, now at £8700, I randomly came across another stock. This was a 'holdings company'. I had no idea what that even meant, but it was on the 'top winners' section (which I had never noticed before) on my trading platform as it was up 90% in one day and was now trading at 14 cents per share. 90% up in one day?! 14 cents a share?! I could've nearly doubled my money if I'd invested in it that morning—within a few hours, too! It baffled me how one stock could climb so high in one day, simply because I didn't know how volatile penny stocks were. I did a tiny bit of research online and, being as naive as I was, threw my whole £8700 into it! A few days, maybe a week later, I hit £10,000. I screamed hysterically; I was rich, I was rich!! Jess rolled her eyes and didn't really understand it because the money was in my trading account and not in my bank. She told me to withdraw it, and so did everyone else. My grandparents told me to get it out as soon as I told them, and so did my mother. They then said the same thing at £20,000, £50,000, £100,000 and £200,000.

It took FIVE WEEKS for my £8700 to become £200,000. Luck? Smart investing? Inside information? Nope. The Law of Attraction, and that's it.

Up until I started investing, I'd earned £30,000 max. that year (£18,000 the year before), mainly through online Personal Training, but as I've said, I only managed to keep around £7000 as I spent a lot on redecorating and the baby! I also bought a BMW X5 that I manifested— forgot to mention that.

In the middle of November, I'd added to my manifestations list. I wanted to earn a little more that year, so I added 'I make £60,000 this year' to my list. I'm not going to lie, I even doubted myself on this one. I realised that I'd basically have to earn £30,000 in

December alone, which is the quietest time for taking on online clients! The Universe really worked with me on this one, as instead of making £30,000 from the point of writing down the manifestation, I made almost £200,000. That's more than Chris Hemsworth made for the first Thor film! What the fuck!

I started becoming a part of a community of shareholders of this company online. People were posting how they'd be able to buy a car from their investments, and I was planning to get into property! My bank balance in January 2020 had been £200!

One of the main reasons I truly believe that the Universe gave me £200,000 that year was because the Universe knew I would also help everyone else I knew to get free money like I was. I told everyone—and I mean everyone—about this company. I posted it online when I reached £22,000 and told people that I had made £14,000 in two weeks. I felt so rich. A lot of people asked about it and what it was, and a lot of people invested too and made thousands. Some people called me a liar and said that if I had earned that much then I wouldn't still be working in a supermarket. I told one friend, and he asked me if I had been hacked and if it was actually me messaging him and even asked me to take a photo with a sock on my head to prove it. He didn't end up believing me, or investing. One friend put £500 in and hit £6000 a few weeks later, two put £5000 in and hit £30,000, and everyone was telling their mates, too. I believe that if this gift that I received/manifested had been given to someone else, the majority would've kept it to themselves. I, on the other hand, was telling everyone, 'If you want free money, do this.' My mother invested, nearly everyone at work invested, and honestly, it felt great. It took nothing out of my pocket and put a lot into others', and it brought me great satisfaction knowing that I could spread the info!

Then the rocket halted. The one stock that I was all in on dropped dramatically (like $2). My £200,000 turned into £84,000 in the same week, awesome. I didn't start doubting the Law of Attraction here, but I was so annoyed and frustrated that my money was falling so fast! I also knew that the Universe gives you what you give it, so me focusing on losing money was only going to bring more loss of money, which annoyed me even more! It was so hard to focus on a mindset that made me feel rich when my money was tumbling! At this point, I didn't even think I'd be able to finish this book!

Another company then came up online that I'd seen a few people talk about, and me being risky as fuck, I put all my money into it. First I think I sold £30,000 worth of my main stock and it doubled fast, then I moved all of my money into it. I think it took three days to hit £231,000, and I knew that I was going to be a millionaire within a month. When my account hit £200,000 again, it took literally less than five minutes to reach £231,000. I sat there with the biggest grin on my face and told myself that once it hit £250,000, I'd take £30,000 out for a car I wanted.

I blinked and it was £187,000.

Then £150,000.

Then £115,000.

Then £100,000.

Yikes.

Have you ever *felt* your hair turn grey? At this point, I was really low and didn't stop looking at my phone for two days, just watching my portfolio plummet. I thought that if I was to sell my shares, it'd just rocket back up and I'd miss it! However, I'd invested £6700 into the market in November, and if you'd have told me back then that in two months I'd have six figures…

I then changed things around, put money into an ISA, diversified and recalculated everything in my mind. I got back up to £200,000 by February 2021 and then withdrew £40,000 and treated myself to a Range Rover Sport, which I'm still in awe of and laugh each time I look out of the window at it. I bought the car just after Piper was born as she was getting heavy, so we needed something with four doors! We also planned to drive to Barcelona with the baby and dogs so it was ideal for us. Although it was a well-deserved treat to myself, I knew that I could always sell it and that would cover our bills for two years if my stocks went tits up!

At the start of this book, I mentioned how I made one million pounds in 45 seconds and then lost it all. What a story I'm about to tell, buckle up. One of the first titles I came up with for this book, even when I only had four figures in the bank, was *25-Year-Old Millionaire*. Around a month before I made my first million, I changed my phone's background to text that read 'I'm a millionaire'. I did this so that every time I opened my phone I'd be drilling the millionaire status into my head over and over again, almost subconsciously.

On social media, there was this one guy who I'd label as a 'guru'; let's call him Bob. Bob had thousands of followers and a big group of people following his calls (investing/stock tips). We got on well for months and talked about property amongst other things. Bob was a Bitcoin millionaire, owned a very nice apartment in a very nice area and was looked up to by everyone. There was a group of us investors, maybe five to ten of us, and Bob would reach out to us and tell us about any new stocks that were about to rocket so we could invest early, even before he told his followers—what a legend, right??

So, this opportunity came up. Bob was contacted by a company that was developing this ground-breaking platform that was the first of its kind, and just before the launch, they'd have a coin (cryptocurrency) that investors could buy into to hopefully profit off. They told Bob that they'd gift him free coins, and in return he'd promote the coin on his social media. Bob told me about the whole thing and he was super excited, which also made me super excited. I was informed that within the first week, this coin should do 10,000%. That's 100x your money. Boy was I pumped. What would I need for a million? £10,000. I calculated that if I invested £10,000, I'd make £1,000,000 in the first week. You may be reading this and thinking that it doesn't sound realistic, but the first big stock I went all in on achieved more than this! I told Bob that I was putting £10k in, and he said he was doing the same.

Around a week later Bob contacted me again. He'd been on the phone to the developers of this platform for over an hour, and his levels of excitement had quadrupled. His prediction doubled to 20,000% in the first week. That's two million for me! Bob decided to invest £25,000 now. So, another week passes, and they're just about to launch the coin, with around five to ten of us getting in first before it being announced to the masses. A mate of mine and I agreed to meet with Bob once we were all millionaires, even though Bob already was one, to celebrate.

When a coin is released, there's only a certain amount available in circulation, and in this case there were 600 million of them. Bob gave me the details as soon as they were available, and in went my £10k—let's do this!

Honestly, within 45 seconds, I was a millionaire. A literal millionaire. My fiancée was crying, my whole body was experiencing a rollercoaster rush, and I couldn't believe it had actually come true. My manifestations, Bob's words, one of my life goals.

Here's where it gets weird.

Somehow, my money got me 89 million coins, which was a lot. I posted online that I had bought the coins and how many I held, and instantly I was bombarded with questions. People were asking if it was MY coin because I held more coins than ANYONE—even more than the developers, even more than Bob. I questioned Bob about it, and he said that I was extremely lucky and I held the most as I'd got in the earliest. I asked him how many he was holding, and the answer was 39 million. It didn't add up.

'How much did you invest, Bob?'

'£3k.'

'I thought you were putting £25k in?'

'I put £3k in and was so busy telling everyone else about how to buy that by the time I went to put more money in, the price was too high.'

Hmm.

I explained that I was actually a millionaire, and then Bob begged me not to sell anything. I owned more coins than anyone, which meant that if I had sold all my coins, the entire thing would come crashing down. Bob had made me an actual millionaire, so of course I was going to listen to him—I had a lot of respect for him. I checked the coin again to see how my million was doing, a mere few minutes later.

£360,000.

I calculated it again, and by the time I did…

£150,000.

Minutes later.

£9000.

'Bob, what's going on?'

'I don't know. I think some of the developers, or some guys that I told have all sold.'

When the price of a stock/coin drops so quickly, a lot of other holders panic and sell their shares/coins, which in turn creates a bigger drop and causes even more panic selling.

My million had gone. Surely it'd go back up though? It was still the first day, of course it would go back up. I was getting a lot of messages that day and the day after. A lot of them were sending me information that made it look like the coin and the platform itself was all a big scam, and some messages were just pure hate and abuse from people thinking that it was all me: my coin, my scam. I told them all it wasn't a scam but really had my doubts. Was Bob scamming me? Surely he wouldn't? Was Bob getting scammed? No, it's all legit, Ben, this stuff happens, it's just people taking profits. The platform was set to launch in a week's time, so I announced online that I felt that things didn't add up, but I was still holding, at least until the platform was out. The thing is, if I was an outsider looking in, I'd 100% think it was all me. I owned more coins than anyone! Of course it looked like me.

The next day, the coin started going back up slightly, and my profit was sitting at around £65,000. I barely slept all night but was starting to feel better. There was no way the Universe would put all that money in front of my face just to almost instantly take it away, right? Then I had another message. Someone had tried logging into the company's account on social media and clicked 'forgot password?'. The page stated something along the lines of:

To retrieve your password, we can send a text to 'this' number or 'this' email.

It was Bob's number.

It was Bob's email.

There was no platform, there were no developers, it was all Bob. It was all a scam. This man that I'd fully trusted knew that I would put money into it and promote it, and took advantage. Bob created the coin himself, and while he was begging me not to sell anything at a million, he was simultaneously selling all of his. A classic 'pump and dump', as they call it.

Before I sold, I called him out about the email and phone number, and he denied it, called it an attack against himself and said he'd sort it. I sold and announced it online. I stated that I panicked after receiving some information and sold. I didn't say it was a scam as the evidence wasn't concrete and I really wanted to believe that Bob was telling the truth. Thousands of people lost all their money, and I was extremely lucky to not lose all mine. As I owned so many coins, I was only able to sell five million at a time. Each time I sold, the price would drop, meaning that each 5 million was worth less than the last. I came out with £11k profit and gave a lot of it to people who I'd told to invest and had lost money. Bob's social media name wasn't even his real name, his apartment wasn't his and he wasn't a millionaire—before the coin anyway. He was a con artist. Bob deleted all of his social media accounts and disappeared with around £600,000. Karma will get him, but how can someone do that to thousands of people, affecting thousands of families and their hard-earned cash? One guy told me he put £30,000 in at the top and lost it all.

It took around a week for the abuse towards me to stop, and after all the evidence came out, my name was cleared.

A millionaire in less than a minute. Imagine one million pounds being placed in your hands and then taken away, mind-boggling. Life-changing money made and lost just like that.

I started questioning it on a deeper level, though. What did it mean? Was there a message there? Stop trusting people? Learn to take profits? Do I actually *need* to be a millionaire? Was I being tested to see how much I truly wanted the money? I then began to question if it was my fault. Had I asked for it wrong? Had I manifested it in the wrong way? At the start of my journey, when I'd tried manifesting that silver Audi A4, it had appeared right outside my house but wasn't mine because I hadn't been specific enough. I'd asked for a million, and all the Universe did was deliver, no questions asked. I didn't manifest *keeping* the million per se. Focusing on the positives helped, but there weren't too many.

During this time and for a little while after, the markets were rough. The majority of stocks were continuously dropping, and it took its toll on everyone's moods. It got to one point where I thought I'd feel like a fraud publishing this book because my portfolio had fallen so low! I deleted my trading app and decided to delve further into the mental aspect of it all. How could I be writing about how to attract wealth and happiness if I'd stopped implementing the techniques in my own life?

I told myself that complaining about losing money would only bring more loss and started acting like the richest man I knew, and lo and behold, everything turned around. The entire market shifted, and a lot of stocks—especially mine—almost literally blew up! Just the flick of a mental shift, and things were that easily put back on track!

***

So, that's me. That's my story, so far. My income is now through dividend stocks, and I'm still debating whether to get into property for a number of reasons. I can't fully believe that I no longer work at the age of 25, have one of my dream cars and am the happiest man I've ever met. I will make a lot more money than I already have, and plan to do very big things to help others.

As I write this section of the book, I'm currently on holiday with Jess, Piper, Romeo and Cooper, and I spent the morning bouncing between writing and reading (and juggling the baby). Before my day started and just after feeding Piper, I jumped into the hot tub and started manifesting. The previous day saw my portfolio drop a little, and the whole market has been rough for everyone. Today, though, I changed the direction. I told myself that I had more money than I did. I felt how good I would feel if I were to have that money, and I looked around and imagined how I'd act and hold myself if I had all that money. A few hours after, the market opened, and it's the best day the market has seen in two or three months and my portfolio climbed 16%. If you keep complaining about losing money then I guarantee that you'll soon lose more. But if you truly believe you have an abundance of it, more is already heading your way!

In one of the sections you're about to go on to read, you'll ask yourself how much money you *actually* need. Once I'm covered completely, have my dream house and a supercar, I won't really need much more money. I already give a lot of money to charity, but I want to do more. I find it crazy how we put water in our irons to get creases out of our clothes, but there are people without that water to drink and even without clothes on their backs. I find it mind-boggling that our governments spend billions on war while there are people dying on our streets of starvation. I'm going to make a change, mark my words.

I honestly hope that my story inspires you and that you can relate to always wanting the best life for yourself and your own family. Throughout the rest of the book, I'll teach you how it's very possible to have every single thing you've ever wished for and more, whilst truly loving each hour that passes. Let's go.

Like I mentioned at the beginning of this book, I won't waffle. The books I've read that have had a tremendous impact on me could've had the same effects in half the pages, so that's my aim here. Some of the methods I'm going to suggest simply will not resonate with you, and that's absolutely fine—you should take it as a sign—but I'd like you to give the majority of them a go and also to keep an open mind. Some are aimed at changing your mindset, positivity and general outlook on life. Some of these teachings and techniques are there to raise your vibration and lift your energy to the same level your goals are on and the same level future-you is already vibrating on. Other techniques are specific to the Law of Attraction and manifesting. I'll add my Twitter at the end of the book, so please don't hesitate to reach out and ask any questions or tell me about your journey.

MORNING ROUTINE

Let us begin where we start, the morning. Nailing your morning routine is crucial, and if you find that your morning is rushed, get up earlier (call me Ben 'The Rock' Cole-Edwards). Since having a newborn baby, the majority of my mornings consist of timing feeds and nappy changes and, if I'm lucky, breakfast. However, on a good day, I spend one to two hours really connecting with myself. Now, this is really easy to say, coming from someone who doesn't work—but trust me, even if it's 15 minutes of 'you time' before the day begins, it'll be worth it. My routine really sets me up for the day, and it will do the same for you. When I was talking about the Law of Attraction earlier, I spoke about how having a good or bad morning will result in a good or bad day. This is why it's crucial to really lay out the rest of your day emotionally, just by implementing a few practices before breakfast.

So, I get up naturally (without an alarm) and have something small to eat, usually a spoonful of peanut butter and an apple, or something similar. If you need to set an alarm, that's absolutely fine, but try to set one that has a relaxing tone to it. What really helps with waking up to an alarm is to hold a big cheesy grin once you open your eyes. Another day to smash those inner goals, another day to connect, another day to see joy. I then sit in the middle of my living room and spend five minutes doing some yoga stretches. I never do what I like to call 'full-on' yoga, but more 'yoga-like' stretches, opening my limbs, ready for the day. Breathing is key here, and I like to fully use my lungs, aaaall the way in, aaaall the way out. I then return to sitting and meditate. Meditating, for me, and for you, can be approached in a variety of ways. It's not just one thing, and not many people realise that. I'm always sat in silence (or with two French Bulldogs snoring), but sometimes I envision my future, sometimes I sit with a wide smile on my face, manually raising my vibration, and sometimes I just sit. Being in a meditation doesn't have to be you chanting, surrounded by candles and twitching as you leave your body. It can literally be you thinking good things, feeling good feelings, or even thinking about absolutely nothing. Each to their own and all that.

Meditation is becoming more and more mainstream, and I love that. People are really starting to connect with themselves, and there's nothing better. Imagine—the Prime Minister could do it!

I then walk the dogs or take the baby for a stroll; Jess isn't an early bird. Sometimes I like to listen to music when walking the dogs, and sometimes I like to take a country route and listen to the wind and birds in the trees. There's one lonely house on a nice route that I normally walk, and I used to use it as a 'checkpoint'. Every time I passed the house, I would tell myself that the next time I pass it, I'll have more money; I started doing this at £19,000. Being out in nature is great, and I especially love it early in the morning. You can hear people heading out to work, and it really does feel like the world is waking up and starting to move, a true sensation of connection.

Early in the morning, I pass a lot of elderly people whilst out walking, and it's very rare that we won't exchange a smile and conversation. Old people are almost always happy and seem so at peace, and it really does pass on.

If I pass someone who doesn't wear a happy look, I'll always try my best to put one on their face. If, like me, you believe that we're all connected via one consciousness, you'll understand how lifting others up will in turn lift you up.

Upon returning home from my walk, I normally do 20-30 minutes of reading and learn a little Spanish! Some days I spend 15 minutes dancing to myself in the mirror—hey ho, whatever floats your boat. Even writing this sounds way too productive for my liking, so believe me when I say this isn't a daily occurrence!

Don't feel disheartened if you can't do all of this every single day, because neither do I. When writing the routine, I had to really stop and think about what the next step was. Shit, I can't even remember the last time I walked past checkpoint house!

SHOWERING

My shower is a tool I use to attract success in all areas of my life. While the warm water's running, after I've washed, I face away from the showerhead and close my eyes. Here I go over my list of affirmations, sometimes in my head, sometimes out loud. I put my arms out in front of me and physically 'pull' my affirmations and goals towards me as I recite them. I can't really explain this movement without it sounding weird, but—imagine there's someone standing in front of you, holding out a tray, or anything for that matter. When reciting each affirmation, put your arms out, take the tray for yourself and bring it into your body. Does that make sense, or are you just imagining a weird school dinner lady showering with you? With each affirmation, I like to take a big breath in. This gives me the sensation that my body is getting bigger/fuller with my goals and makes me want to run 100 miles and smash every single target I have. Before exiting the shower, I switch the water to as cold as it will go and usually last 5-10 seconds before jumping out. This shocks your body and really makes you feel 'awake'. Notice how I used quotes there? Two meanings.

With two dogs and a baby, the shower is one area that I can really calm my mind with zero distractions, usually. Think of it as an affirmation accelerator that you can step into and step out of as a new person. This takes us nicely into the next lesson.

BE THE PERSON YOU WANT TO BE

You can literally step out of the shower as the new person that you so wish to be. Like some dimensional *Stars in Their Eyes*, if you will. You want to be a person on top of their finances? Switch the shower off and tell yourself that the second you step out of it, you'll be that person who is on top of their finances. Want to always be in a good mood and not let anyone get to you? Want to be filthy rich? Step out of the shower and vibrate on that level, and it'll come to you quicker than you could imagine. How would that person walk? How would that person hold themselves? Would you constantly be smiling if you were a millionaire? Then get out of the shower and show the world that smile (get dressed first, though).

This doesn't have to be limited to the shower, however. Sometimes if I need to go shopping, I'll *be* the person that I want to be. If I want to be a multimillionaire, I'll walk like one. If someone looks at me, they're looking at me because they know I'm a multimillionaire. This is almost a mental 'fake it until you make it'. If you had told me to do this two years ago, I would've laughed, but I'm telling you because it's worked and continues to work so well for me. I'm doing it now—I'm currently a *New York Times* Best Selling Author.

NEGATIVITY

Negativity and doubt can physically and emotionally break a person.

'I'm going to university!'

'Why don't you become a doctor?'

'I've just written my first novel!'

'I didn't like it.'

'I'm going to be a Personal Trainer!'

'Haha, you don't know what you're doing.'

'I've started a clothing brand!'

'Why would people buy clothes from you?'

'I've just started investing!'

'That's gambling; you'll lose it all.'

'I've just made a quarter of a million pounds in two months!'

'Any tips?'

Family doubted me, friends laughed at me, colleagues made fun of me, and strangers on the internet bullied me for doing something that wasn't nine-to-five. Do you know what they're doing now? Reading this book for advice.

I became like an actual fucking superhero when I mastered the ability to control my emotions, and guess how long that took me? Seconds. I want you to read the following four words until they sink in, embed themselves into your brain and change your life:

YOU CONTROL YOUR EMOTIONS.

That's it, that's the secret. If you take away one thing from this book, please, let it be that. Go back and read it again. Someone says something that has the potential to upset you? YOU control your emotions. You didn't get paid the amount you thought you would, and now you can't buy what you wanted? YOU control your emotions. Your boss has been giving you a hard time? YOU control your emotions. No one else can alter your state of mind, and no one else can bring your mood down once you understand this. Do you remember a time when someone said something to you that upset you? Were you rejected by someone, and that caused sadness? Did you apply for something and didn't get accepted, sending you on a downward spiral? As harsh as it sounds, that was all on you. You let all external things in and all emotions out in any which way you want, did you know that? So you didn't get into the university that you wanted to? Smile, it wasn't for you. Something better awaits.

We all have family members that say something negative during almost every visit, even if they don't mean to. That's definitely the case for me, and I know they won't read this, as they won't understand why I'm writing a book—unless it makes a lot of money they can share of course. It got to the point that any time I'd visit certain members of the family, I'd just wait for them to say something to put me down. This was also a lot to do with the Law of Attraction. In my mind, I knew they'd say something that I wouldn't like, so the Universe always agreed with me and delivered just that. In the end, I made a game of it—Ooh, what will they say *this* time! Treasure your emotions.

Here's a metaphor for you (if that's even the word for it): your emotional state is a house. Nice and warm inside, with plenty of windows to see the world outside. Someone who says/does something that can affect your mood is a burglar trying to break into the house. There are several windows and two doors, which gives them plenty of ways to get in. Keep your lights shining bright within, and a good security system and they won't be able to get in! Fuck me, that analogy (ah, that's the word) sounded a lot better in my head.

Top tip: A person will only try and bring you down if they are below you.

AFFIRMATIONS

This is up there as one of the best/main techniques that'll help you progress the quickest. Don't forget: the Universe is just waiting for you to connect with it and work with it. Once you decide what you want and ask the Universe for it, the Universe becomes excited and simply cannot wait to get started and help you out. The Universe has always been working with you, but once you 'click' and *understand* that—lightspeed.

But what exactly *are* affirmations? Google says, 'The act or process of affirming something.' Sounds simple, right? 'So I just say something about myself and then keep saying it?' Precisely! Like, honestly. Do you doubt that? Do you doubt that simply saying something over and over can have a drastic effect on your life? Then how are you reading this book? Because I manifested my affirmations of it.

Affirmations can be done in a number of ways: out loud, in your head, written down, in the shower, whilst driving or whilst meditating. The possibilities are endless, but you need to experiment and find out which way works best for you. There are no wrong options here. My first affirmations started to come true and appear in my physical reality after around a week of thinking about them for five minutes a day. So don't think that you'll have to wait months for things to happen. The more you believe and the more you trust the process and put your faith in the Universe, the quicker the results will appear.

I started by saying them in my head when reading certain books. The books would tell me to write down my affirmations, and I was literally too lazy to do so. As I've already stated, when I started reading and learning about the Law of Attraction it was very warm in the UK (somehow) and I spent most of my time in the garden. When the books would tell me to write things down, there was no way I was going to get up off of the garden furniture, head inside the house to find a pen and notepad, return to the garden and then write things down just to read them out in my head. I thought that saying them in my head would have the same effect. Every book kept repeating how important it was to put pen to paper and it took me a good few weeks to start writing.

My first affirmations weren't spot on, and the way they manifested wasn't how I wanted. For example, I was imagining the silver Audi A4 outside my house, and within days one appeared outside the house, but it wasn't mine. When I started writing my affirmations, however, things changed rapidly.

Here's a little more about that.

I'd begin my writing journey by stating regular things that were actually already true: I am Ben Cole-Edwards, I am happy, I am healthy, I have the perfect relationship with Jess, we have two healthy dogs at home, Romeo and Cooper. Then, in between these statements, I'd add a sentence that would state something that I *wanted*, but written as though I already had it. For example:

- I'm Ben Cole-Edwards
- I have financial freedom
- I am happy
- I make £60,000 this year
- I have the perfect relationship with Jess
- I have an Audi R8

Etc.

Etc.

The 'trick' here, if you will, is fooling your brain. This is something that still baffles me, because how can your brain fool your brain? Look, if something isn't broken, don't fix it; it works. The funny thing is, your brain doesn't know the difference between reality and your imagination. So, if you're reading through your list of affirmations as though they're all already true and you really do believe it, then your brain will not know the difference. You move from reading words on a piece of paper to actually conditioning your brain into believing that your future goals have already been achieved. You are literally aligning yourself with the life that you desire and raising your vibration to match your dreams. Everything you want is already there, but it's just vibrating on a higher frequency than you currently are. Do you want to be a millionaire? Act like one. Do you want to own a Ferrari? Imagine how you'd feel owning a Ferrari, and feel like that 24/7. Please, trust me, I am living proof of this. I used the same techniques that Conor McGregor and Jim Carrey used. I would drive around in a £600 car and imagine it was a supercar and imagine how it would feel. I'd physically feel the car drop lower and imagine the interior changing. I'd drive through town and imagine everyone turning their heads to look at the car. The first car that I wanted to own once I made money was a 2014 Range Rover Sport with a certain body kit on it. Something sporty, luxurious and family sized that would own the road. I bought one, two weeks before I wrote this sentence, in cash.

Jim Carrey once wrote himself a cheque for ten million dollars and kept it in his wallet. I may be mistaken on the timeframe here, but I believe he wrote the cheque in 1985 and dated it for ten years later, with it reading 'acting services rendered'. Ten years later, he got paid ten million dollars for *Dumb & Dumber*. That's it. That's all you need to know. This is all you need to read. Should this paragraph be the blurb?

Anything you set your mind to is possible. Anything. The secret ingredients are you, belief and frequency.

WHERE IS YOUR HAPPINESS?

After all the reading I've done, something that has really fixed itself into my brain is regarding where your happiness is. There's no beating around the bush here, but if you're waiting for a holiday/car/new purchase/the weekend to be happy, then you'll be living miserably in autopilot until a set date. When that date finally arrives, you'll feel happy and you'll feel as though a void has been filled, but that feeling fades away, doesn't it? Within a few days, you've already set your next happiness date, and you'll switch back to autopilot until that day comes. It's very important to have the dates/goals in mind and even more so when they're associated with great emotions, but your happiness isn't in a material thing—it's in YOU!

If we are constantly waiting on our next thing to bring us joy then we are never truly happy. 'Gee, doesn't life go quick.' YES! Because you're not living it! You need to appreciate and become happy with every single moment of every single day to feel true happiness, regardless of what's going on around you and regardless of what material things you have in your life. Stop just 'getting by' and living parallel to each day, and open your eyes to see that you *are* each day. Happiness is a feeling, not a place or thing—understand that. If you know what you think you *need* to be happy, then you can kill two birds with one stone. Let's say you really want to go on a holiday and you just *know* that you'll be happy as soon as you step off that plane and feel that heat. You know the exact way you'll feel at that time, so choose to feel that now, not just then. Doing this means that not only will you be in a constant state of gratitude (for the imaginary heat and week away that you're now feeling) but also you'll be telling the Universe that a holiday will bring you joy, and the Universe will bring it to you even quicker.

DO YOU *ACTUALLY* WANT TO BE A MILLIONAIRE?

The main reason you picked this book up is due to the fact that you desire financial freedom, and that's great, but have you ever asked yourself, or even calculated, how much money that really is? Personally, at this point in time, I have enough money in one stock that pays dividends, enough of a payout each quarter, that my bills and my partner's bills are covered. So, this money allows me to no longer need to work to cover my bills, and it's not actually that much. I could've sold all my shares after three weeks of investing and quit my jobs then and been covered, but—you guessed it—I wanted more.

But what if you're like me and enjoy holidays and cars and have a spending problem? Let's add that up based on my own current goals.

- Four bedroom house with a drive and garden - £250,000-£300,000
- Supercar - £35,000-£60,000

With decorating the house and a few other things, that's under £500,000. Half a million. After that point, the dividend-paying stock covers my bills, and anything extra allows for holidays and purchases. So for me, I don't *need* millions to live a more-than-comfortable life, and if you calculate your own individual goals, you may come to realise the same thing. The two things in my list are actually not necessary at all, meaning I don't even need all that money. One of the best dividend stocks I know of will pay around £20,000-£30,000 a year for a £200,000 investment. £200,000 is a lot of money, I know. If you don't think it is, then consider yourself lucky! When I began this whole journey, I would never have even dreamt of having that kind of money, and now I've had times where I've lost that kind of money over the space of a week and it's not even phased me.

Wonderful, truly wonderful things can happen when you believe in the process and practise these teachings. Even £100,000 in a stock like that would be £10,000-£15,000 a year, which is a decent wage in my area. Really add up what you actually *need*, not want, and I guarantee you'll be surprised.

DO WHAT BRINGS YOU JOY!

One of the best and easiest things you can do to raise your vibration and pull yourself out of a negative space is to just do something that brings joy. This is my favourite and most used technique to align myself with the Universe to allow myself to receive my desires. What makes you happy? What brings you joy, puts a warm feeling in your belly and a nice little smile on your face? Dancing? Listening to music? Writing? Reading? Walking? Meeting friends? Animals? Gaming? I don't want to quote Nike here, but...

For me, there are two things that really help to make me feel happy, both in different ways. Number one? Lego. I fucking love Lego. Last week I spent 11 hours putting together a Lego Jeep, and I was in my absolute element. I've enjoyed building Lego all my life (and then it gathers dust), and it really takes me back to being a child. Do you know what a child worries about? How to get their hands on more Lego, that's it. It's something that calms me, keeps me occupied, takes my mind off anything that's bothering me—and also, Lego is awesome. If I reeeally want to calm my mind, besides meditating, Pokémon is great too.

My second go-to is music. Yesterday I was woken up by a text that really pissed me off, and I let it piss me off. I wound myself up and went over imaginary conversations in my head to annoy myself even further. Using the 'Choose Again Method', a technique by a favourite author of mine, Gabrielle Bernstein, I chose my second go-to mood enhancer to pick myself up again, starting my morning the right way and setting myself up for the rest of the day. Alexa, play something by Queen. Music really gets me in a good mood. Whether it's singing, dancing or just vibing, I feel like I really tune-in to each song and allow upbeat music to uplift me and feed my soul. Alexa, play 'All Night Long' by Lionel Richie. Have you ever woken up to that song? Makes you feel as though you're on holiday, about to hit the beach!

On the opposite side of this, and quite obvious actually: don't keep doing something that *doesn't* bring you joy. This relates to, but isn't limited to: jobs, being in a certain place and being around certain people. When I was in the factory job that I was getting bullied in, I understood this concept and stopped letting the bullies have any of my time, simply because it wasn't benefitting me and was not bringing me joy. I'd always laugh and brush off what they were saying, but as soon as I stopped smiling, or even responding, they had nothing to bounce off and very quickly stopped. That brought me joy. This also relates to changing things up when you're in a bad mood and not feeling joy. If something has annoyed you and you're slouching on the sofa, watching TV, guess what? You're going to stay annoyed, you won't really watch what's in front of you and you'll waste precious time being in a state of mind that'll only bring you more of the same thing. Get up, move around, take control of your emotions, your mood, and find that which brings you joy!

Before moving on to the next section of this book, I want you to really have a good think about what brings you joy. Write it down if you have to so you can look back on it. If you find yourself deep in a bad mood, do what brings you joy, and you'll find yourself quickly climbing out of that hole you've dug.

BE SELFISH

Short and sweet with this one here. You've heard this time and time again throughout your life. Your teachers in school will have told you, your parents will have told you, and now I am going to tell you. **Nobody is going to do it for you.** That's that, that's it. A lot of people may *help* you, but let me tell you, it's extremely rare to find someone that will help you get more than what they've got themselves. Let that sink in. Your boss in work may help you, push you and motivate you to get a promotion, but they won't help you to take their own job or go above them. You've just got to do you. I'm a little different actually, and once I started investing I posted a lot about certain stocks online and made some people a lot more than I made myself, happily. It's an amazing feeling to give help to others, whether that's knowledge or even a hug, and you should never be afraid to ask for help— just pick your mentors wisely. It's great to help other people, but always remember to put number one first.

SOCIAL MEDIA

Focusing on where others are will stop you from focusing on where you're going. Read that again.

Let's start by talking about how depressing social media can be—and more specifically, who you follow. Social media, for me, is 90% money/mindset and 10% memes, and I only tend to follow people who motivate me and inspire me. What's very important to understand though, is that 99% of the accounts that you follow are *definitely* highlight reels. Think about it, if you were a social media 'influencer' who posts photos to promote clothes and products, purely for income purposes, why would you post about the debt you're struggling with or the issues within your relationship? That's what you don't see. Allowing yourself to look into the life of the rich can be very depressing and can make you forget how far you've already come.

Something I heard a while back really stuck with me, and it's this:

'Don't compare someone's chapter 20 to your chapter 1.'.

If you pick up the third instalment of the Harry Potter books, he's already a talented wizard. Unless you've followed his whole story, you don't know about his struggles, everything he's had to overcome, his obstacles and everything he's lost; you just see him now. And yeah, I just used 'The Boy Who Lived' to put that into context for you. It's true though, and the same can be said for the people you follow and possibly look up to on social media. I'm not suggesting you should have a social media detox (although that is an extremely beneficial thing to do), but just take a look at who you're following and ask yourself if you enjoy seeing them on your feed. Do you enjoy their posts? *That's fine.* Do their posts benefit or motivate you? *That's great.* Do their posts make you envious? *Not so good.*

In the words of Mark Manson, 'You only have so many fucks to give, so you need to choose what you give a fuck about.' Let them do them. You do you.

GIVING

If someone asked me what the key is to receiving an abundance of what you desire, my answer would be the title here: giving. Giving is the key to receiving, without a doubt. By giving to others, be it money, a helping hand or even advice, you tell the Universe that with everything it gives you, you also give back.

Like I've said previously in this book, one of the main reasons that the Universe handed me all my money so easily was because it knew that I'd help others accumulate wealth too. After my first week of investing, I told others online about the main stock I was in and how it was going to change my life. A lot of people, including family, told me not to tell anyone about it and to keep it all to myself. First, it was taking zero money out of my pocket, and secondly, why not? Even people who weren't very nice to me in school have profited from following my social media pages and copying what I've done.

Abraham Hicks (please read his teachings next if you haven't already) teaches that our sole purpose here on Earth is to find joy. Many people state that money can't buy happiness, but I believe that it does, and if I can help others find joy in life whilst taking nothing away from mine then I'm a very happy man. I frequently get people contacting me to thank me for making them money and for switching them on to the Law of Attraction. I see so many of my followers understand and open their eyes to the inner workings of the Universe as I explain it to them, and then I see them posting about it themselves and spreading the word. I love that. Giving all my knowledge regarding happiness-building can only spread joy throughout the world. I'm basically the Benai Lama.

GRATITUDE

Being grateful is something that isn't practised and expressed enough, even by myself until recently. Before I started this whole journey and before I started writing this book, all I wanted was more. I wanted more money, a nicer car, a nicer house, and that was one of the main reasons why I didn't have more of what I wanted. For the Universe to bring you what you desire, you have to be in alignment with it. The Universe listens to your words, your thoughts and your feelings, but above all else it responds to your vibrational frequency. If you're on the frequency of 'want', where you are only desiring more than you currently have, then you are really on the frequency of 'lack'. You are telling the Universe what you are lacking. 'I want more money' becomes 'I have a lack of money', 'I want a bigger house' becomes 'I hate this house'. Unfortunately, all this does is bring more 'lack'. The Universe reads your frequency and your energy and understands that your constant mood is wanting more, so it simply brings you more of that. If you constantly complain that your monthly pay isn't enough for you to live on, then it will never be enough.

It's well and truly great to want more in life, don't get me wrong. Again, our purpose here in life is to find joy, and if the things that you want more of bring you joy then surely you're on the right path? That's half correct, yes. But you also need to be honestly happy and grateful for your current situation. Being content with your finances, your job, your house and your life overall, even when it's all falling apart, tells the Universe that you're happy with everything but also happy to welcome in what you desire. The Universe feels the smile on your face when you look at your children, it feels the happiness and excitement you feel when you receive money, and it reacts by giving you more of that. *Sarah seems to be loving money and it really does bring her joy to know she's secure and can travel when she pleases. Let's give her more of that!*

When I was working in the supermarket, I rarely had more than £200 spare, and especially when I first started, I would always beg for overtime. There were a few members of staff that I just didn't get on with, and it created a bad energy around the place in my mind, which I was unknowingly sending out to the Universe. I wanted more hours to work so I could get more money, telling the Universe I was lacking money, and I was also always expecting some kind of conflict of interest between a colleague or two and I. Do you know what the Universe did? Brought me more of it! More lack of money and more conflict. So, do you know what I did? I changed it! I flipped the whole thing on its head. One of the shifts that I'd work would start at 5 p.m. and finish late. The late start meant that I would spend all day working myself into a bad mood, ready to start. What I did to change this was to do things that brought joy and look for the things I was grateful for. I had a job that was up the road, and I was so grateful to try my best to make everyone I encountered smile. I made it my mission to not only find joy but to bring joy to others and to see how many laughs I could get out of strangers. Before I'd leave the house for work, I'd perform my shower routine, affirmations, and step out as a new man. I'd then spend

15-20 minutes dancing to some great songs in the mirror, really getting myself in a good mood, setting up a good shift for myself. I used to head to work and see a big list of things to do and that alone would knock my energy down a notch or two, but I realised that my shift would end at a certain time regardless of whether there was one thing to do or thirty, so there was no need to act like a bigger workload would result in staying longer. I started singing as I walked into work, and it really did spread joy and put smiles on other people's faces—not just because of my singing voice either.

Here's something I do that helps in every aspect of my life. Before I go to sleep and just after I wake up, I go over a list of things in my head that I'm grateful for, usually with a big smile on my face. It is the one hundred percent truth when I tell you that I can feel myself physically raising my vibrational frequency. I make my energy and being match my goals vibrationally so I attract them quicker. You can spend hours with your list of gratitude, if you really think about it. Some people go further and further into debt each month with no money spare, while you have enough to buy a book whenever you please—which you probably purchased from your smartphone that costs a few hundred too!

It doesn't even have to be that deep. You could recite your list whilst in bed watching TV, and be grateful for the warm bed that you're on, the soft pillows under your head, and the TV in front of you. Think of how many people don't even have those luxuries. You're here, reading this book to progress further financially and spiritually; you're on the exact path that you were always meant to be on, so be grateful for that.

I only spend a few minutes and go over the main things that I'm grateful for. It goes something like this:

'I am so grateful for my beautiful daughter.

I am so grateful for my perfect fiancée.

I am so grateful for my two healthy dogs, Romeo and Cooper.

I no longer have to work and I am so thankful to be able to spend each day doing whatever I want.

Thank you for my wealth and the ability to help others.

Thank you for the house that I live in and the food that I eat.

I am so grateful to own the car that I own.

Thank you for working with me 24/7 and bringing joy into my life each day.'

The joy I feel when going through my list is almost like a full-body tingle that really does raise my energy. The feeling I get allows me to fall asleep with a smile on my face, a happy mind and a warm heart. Repeating this exercise in the morning before I get out of bed sets me up for the day in the same way. Waking up and practising gratitude will allow you to see the good in the world, not just as a whole but in every single thing you see and every single moment you live in.

VISUALISATION

Being able to visualise my future in the past created my present. (That does make sense, if you read it twice!) I was able to drive around in a £600 car and visualise myself driving around in a Lamborghini. I could feel myself sitting lower, the Lambo badge on the steering wheel and the roar of the engine. I would even turn my music up and put the windows down when driving through town for people to look at me, but I'd imagine that they were looking because it was a supercar that caught their attention.

Before I bought my current car, I'd look at adverts for the model and really take in all the details of the steering wheel so I could imagine myself holding it and envision myself behind the wheel, sat in the car outside my house. It worked a treat! After I bought my Range Rover and was driving it home, I looked down at the steering wheel and clicked. I laughed out loud and said to myself, 'What the fuck?! How did I go from selling my £600 car because I could barely afford to run it, to paying for one of my dream cars two years later in cash?!'

The key here really is to trick your brain into believing that you already have what you want. Like I said, the brain cannot differentiate between imagination and reality. If you fully, one-hundred-and-ten percent believe that you're driving that fancy car, living in that house with a sea view or looking at seven figures in your bank account, even when that's not true, then you will well and truly begin to vibrate on a higher frequency and your inner energy will be sky high. And as we've already learned, the Universe responds to the frequency and level of energy that you're currently providing it, so in turn It will bring you more of the same!

One of my most bizarre visualisations was almost at the very start of this journey and was a technique that I created myself. This technique and the materialisation of it genuinely blew my mind, so I've saved it to mention here. For two weeks straight, I would wake up in the morning, have a cup of tea and sit at my dining table. Whilst sat down and after a few breathing exercises, I would play 'What A Wonderful World' by Louis Armstrong and close my eyes to begin my visualisation. There was a house for sale in a gorgeous area around a thirty minute drive away from my home. It had three storeys, a stunning view of the sea and was in the perfect spot. The house was £950,000, which was about £949,999 out of my budget, but nonetheless, I tried to manifest it. I wasn't specific—which showed when it manifested— but what I did was imagine myself sitting on the balcony of that exact house, looking at the sea whilst drinking my tea and listening to the same song. I performed this technique throughout the duration of the song every morning. As I approached the third week, I headed out to a home where I was booked by a couple for massages. The three of us were chatting and the man explained how the factory he owned had got involved in creating personal protection equipment for the virus and his profits were through the roof. Whilst massaging his partner, she explained how she wanted to book me in for a massage every two weeks, which I was over the moon with, as she would be my first recurring client!

She then went on to say that the only issue would be that they were moving homes in a few months and asked if I'd be able to travel a little further. They showed me their new house. It was the EXACT house that I'd been manifesting. It was the £950,000 house. I freaked out internally and just froze. I was going to be in THAT house, I could sit on THAT balcony and I bet she'd offer me THAT cup of tea, too! I couldn't believe it. I hadn't manifested or envisioned that it was my house, just that I was in the house, and that's exactly what the Universe delivered. I truly felt the Universe at this point, and it was almost literally talking to me.

Another big thing happened when I really committed to manifesting a visualisation—all before I even started learning about this myself. My grandfather was in hospital after getting hit with five different things at once. I'm not going to pull on your heart strings again here, but after a few nights in the hospital, a nurse called my grandmother, auntie, mother and me into a small room. She described the situation and explained that my grandfather would not be leaving hospital and was close to his time. This completely shook my world, as he was the rock of the family who'd helped me so much. The next day, I was walking to the gym to train clients and I was listening to Queen, his favourite band. I phoned Jess halfway there and broke down on the phone. I told her that I simply couldn't lose him, and that's when I decided to take matters into my own hands. I switched to 'We Are the Champions' and as my second favourite Freddie began to sing, I altered my reality from within.

I said to myself, 'No, this isn't going to happen. This is not how we lose him.' I planned it out in my head. It was a Thursday, and I told myself that my grandfather was going to recover over the weekend, the doctor would see him Monday, and he'd be sent home on Wednesday. I was about ten minutes into training my first client, and he could see that I had been upset and he asked how my grandfather was doing. I explained what the nurse had said the day before, and he told me to go home, so I did. I cancelled the rest of my clients for the day, and once visiting time arrived, I headed to the hospital.

My grandfather had been hallucinating and told me how throughout the night he'd been upstairs in the hospital getting supplies with his mate from the army. He hadn't left his bed all night. I explained to him that this wasn't it for him and that he was going to be okay.

'You'll have the weekend to recover, the doctor will check on you Monday and you'll be discharged on Wednesday. I'll pick you up on Wednesday.'

'I hope you're right, Buddy.'

The weekend came and my grandfather got a lot better. The doctor performed his checks on Monday and was happy that his levels were returning to normal. He was discharged on the Wednesday, and I received the phone call to go and pick him up. He got in the car, and as I told him, 'I told you so,' his favourite song played on the radio. That was the Universe, as clear as day, introducing itself to my conscious mind and showing me that I was in fact the one in control.

ABUNDANCE

Here's something we all struggle with—and me especially, at the beginning of my journey. Abundance means an infinite supply and some of my early affirmations were, 'I have an abundance of money' and 'I have an abundance of clients'. The thing is, when writing those down, I just meant that I personally wanted an infinite stream of cash, but there is an abundance of everything for everyone, which I didn't really grasp. When I became a certified Massage Therapist, I was so scared to see the woman who I used to go to for massages. I had it in my head that she obviously hated me as I could potentially be taking her clients. I think I felt this way because that's how I would feel whenever I'd see someone posting online that they had just started a career in my profession.

After a few months, I saw my old Massage Therapist at my supermarket job, and she was so lovely, and I panicked so much that it was all fake and deep down she hated me. Not long after that, she messaged me to book herself in for a massage. She said I could go to her studio and wouldn't need to use my own towels or even oil. I got there and confessed straight away. I told her I thought she hated me, and she laughed and said that she loved that I was now doing what she was doing, as if some of her clients came to me she'd have more free time! I'd been so quick to judge based on my own inner feelings and how I would've reacted, but after that my mind completely changed. I even started helping others become Personal Trainers and told them all my tips and tricks for getting started and getting clients, all for free.

There truly is an abundance of everything and for everyone, so don't think just because someone you know is earning a lot of money that equates to them taking some of your future money. It just doesn't work like that! See someone online posting a photo of a car they've just bought that you've always wanted? Imagine how many more of that make and model there are.

I've mentioned a few times that I strongly believe that we're all 'one'. This means that if you see someone else doing well and start rooting for them, you'll bring that same success towards yourself. In the words of the great Troy Bolton: We're all in this together.

Mentally, that's all it takes. I'm not a guru and there are hundreds of better (and unnecessarily lengthier) books out there, but this is what worked for me and will definitely work for you. Just like the Universe itself, all I want is for you to succeed, for you to attract each and every one of your desires and live the life of your dreams. If you win, we all win.

FINANCES

First, you should know that I am the furthest thing from a financial advisor that you could possibly get, but I do know a thing or two that's worth sharing. As you're already aware, I used to be awful with money; dreadful, if you will. I got into some bad habits, spent more than I earned and took out loans and finance like they were Monopoly money. My credit score almost went negative, and I was constantly broke. Every month I'd be behind with at least one bill, all the way from my first job to my last. Now, however, I'm great with money, and not just because I have more. At this point in my life, I am spending less than I ever did back when I was working, and I even pay my partner's bills, too! Spending is where I—like a lot of youngsters these days—unfortunately got it all wrong.

Like when I left university and took out that £10,000 loan that I 100% did not need. The £259 a month repayment was 'easy' for me to afford, and that mindset then slowly took a hold of me. I was looking for things that I could finance that would add up to my pay each month. What's funny is that now I see people doing the same thing and see how stupid it looks. I know kids these days (my age or slightly younger—not sure why I say kids!) that are literally spending £300-£400 on car finance, £150 on insurance, £25 on tax and £60 on their phone bills each month, right? That's £535-£635 PER MONTH. That's more than I paid for two holidays last year. Like, literally.

Most of this again, I believe, has a lot to do with social media and people trying too hard to impress others, and that's not me being judgemental at all. When I took out the loan and bought a car for £5000, I posted the car online and thought how cool I'd look, how much money I'd look like I was making and how fast the car was compared to others. What I didn't post was the £259 loan, £150 insurance and fuel/tax costs!

Let's have a look at how much money you really have. Let's assume that you're still living at home, working a minimum wage job and doing 40 hours a week, right? If you're living in your own place, good on you, just incorporate your bills. Depending on your age, you'll be earning around £1150 after deductions. Let's say you're not spoiled and pay lodge or towards rent, you pay for your own food and you have a car:

- Lodge: £100
- Car insurance: £80
- Fuel: £100
- Phone bill: £30
- Groceries: £150
- Total: £460

This leaves you with £690 a month! These calculations won't apply to everyone, but you get the idea. It applied to me back in the day, and I had no idea where I was spending all my money. When I lived with my father, he also questioned where my money was going and I couldn't figure it out. I went through my bank statements, and it all slowly added up. I'm sure for one or two months I was spending around £300 on McDonald's! The majority of the time, you're spending money that you don't have to impress people that you don't like, and that's really all it comes down to. You have no real reason to be spending money like your life depends on it, trust me on this one. If I had started investing back then instead of blowing it all on Big Macs, I'd have written this book years ago, probably whilst out in Hawaii.

I am actual, living proof that these techniques and teachings truly work, and my sole purpose in writing them down for you is to help you attain and achieve every single thing that your wonderful mind can conjure up and, ultimately, find your joy.

When I began implementing the practices and using the techniques that I'm sharing with you in this book, things started rapidly falling into place. Within days I could see my manifestations appear, and it was truly like magic. My first 'major' breakthrough took me around five minutes of one technique every morning for two weeks. This was a massive turning point for me. At the beginning of my journey, I believed in coincidences, so a lot of things I was actually manifesting I tried to cover up in disbelief as a coincidence. There are no coincidences.

Please, for your own good, practise one or more of the methods I've mentioned every day. You may 'click' within a few hours, as the Universe is just raring to go and eager to work with you to fulfil your dreams, or it may take a week or two. As long as your mind, eyes and ears are open to the concept of the Universe listening and responding to your energy, frequency and every desire, nothing can go wrong. What's the worst that can happen?

Again, I love hearing from people all over the world who have been inspired by the teachings that I pass on, so please don't hesitate to reach out to me on social media for any guidance or just to let me know how your journey is going.

I truly wish every single one of you all the best in your journey and really, really hope that I've helped. Remember, this book is in your hands for a reason!

Thanks a million.

Ben Cole-Edwards

AUTHOR PROFILE

Ben Cole-Edwards is a mindset expert and certified Life Coach. One of Ben's major aims in life is to spread his knowledge regarding the Law of Attraction, Manifesting and Affirmations to everyone he can, allowing others to find their own happiness and achieve everything they've ever desired.

Twitter: @coachbce

PUBLISHER INFORMATION

Rowanvale Books provides publishing services to independent authors, writers and poets all over the globe. We deliver a personal, honest and efficient service that allows authors to see their work published, while remaining in control of the process and retaining their creativity. By making publishing services available to authors in a cost-effective and ethical way, we at Rowanvale Books hope to ensure that the local, national and international community benefits from a steady stream of good quality literature.

For more information about us, our authors or our publications, please get in touch.

www.rowanvalebooks.com
info@rowanvalebooks.com

CPSIA information can be obtained
at www.ICGtesting.com
Printed in the USA
LVHW091107210821
695688LV00001B/1

9 781913 662592